Reflections in My 20's

Searching for Meaning

Books by Randi-Mae

Coming soon

Veneration in Daily Life:
Honouring Every Moment

Veneration in Daily Life
Poetry

Reflections in My 20's

Searching for Meaning

By: Randi-Mae Stanford-Leibold

Reflections of My 20's
Searching for Meaning

Published by Randi-Mae
Stanford-Leibold
Ajax, Ontario, Canada
www.randimae.com

Copyright© 2016 Randi-Mae Stanford-Leibold

First printing June 2016
ISBN 978-0-9952256-0-2

Dedication

Dedicated to all of the people who have been teachers in my life, the seen and unseen. The ones that pushed me, made me question, forced me to stop, reflect and look within, giving me the desire to live a life of exploration.

This book is a compilation of my reflections in my late 20's. Work, life, love, dreams, adventure and opportunities to grow. I wanted to share my thoughts and experiences with whoever it may help along the way. I truly believe that if we share our journeys with one another we all benefit. We are all here in this moment to grow and experience. I don't know it all, but I can share with you, where I have been.

Through my daily reflections I discovered the word veneration. I now hold it near to my heart. At the end of each reflection there is a question or a call to action to journal and ponder on your own experience. I believe that we can take time to honour all of our moments even the ones that are challenging. May your journey be filled with many experiences that help you grow, and may you learn from every experience enabling you to become your authentic self.

Contents

Simply Listen

*"Be still and listen with your heart,
for there is much to learn in the
present moment."*

Human beings that already exist in this
world, and those who are waiting to enter,
and even those who are waiting to exit have
a story. If we take the time to listen to the
unique stories that shape these beings, we
will find that we all collectively have
something to offer.

Our lives touch and change not just our
own but many. At times we can see where
we have impacted lives and made change.
Other times we feel defeated and believe
perhaps we were better off never embarking
on a painful or tumultuous relationship or
situation. Every moment shapes and shifts
us. More often than not it has a ripple effect
on all things around us. The mood in a
room, how people feel when they are with
us and the series of events that follow.
Every moment awake and asleep is a snap
shot in our existence.

If we slow down enough during the day, we
can witness and engage in those little
frames of the documentary of our life that is

being recorded in our minds and universe regardless of if we actively pay attention or not. Slowing down enough to listen to the sounds that surround us. Taking a moment to engage in a conversation free of time, reminder chimes from our phones, emails, text messages and meetings. This is becoming to sound cliché at this time in the world. The truth is, we miss so much when we allow only a toe or a foot to be present, while all the other body parts are busy doing something else. You can change your life and those around you by simply listening.

Veneration in daily life: Engage in a conversation and be present. Allow the conversation to flow until it naturally comes to an end. Turn your phone off. Take your watch off. No exceptions. Even if you are the CEO of a billion-dollar company. Or an executive director of an underfunded non-profit agency. Be free to have a conversation with someone you know or someone you don't know. Listen to someone's story uninterrupted.

Slowing Down in the Fast Lane

*"Embrace the delays, they too
are a part of your story."*

It's a beautiful day in the middle of
summer. The roads are dry and the sky is
clear. You're driving along the highway
cruising at 130 km's an hour. In the
distance you can see a car that you are
approaching quickly. You can average speed
pretty well, and you know this car is going
slow. You're already trying to think about
how you can maneuver around this car or
tail gate the vehicle until the driver feels
forced to get out of the way. You are now
right behind this car and it is forcing you to
drive at 100 km's an hour. You look around
frantically and try to find a way out. You are
now flustered and agitated. The music that
you were singing along with is no longer
soothing. It has become annoying and you
have turned it off. There is nowhere to turn,
there are cars everywhere going so fast that
you cannot make a lane change. Now you
are stuck for about 4 km's behind this
vehicle. You drive by a sign that says
maximum speed 100 km/h. Right after the
sign there is a police officer with the radar

gun out pulling cars over. Was the car in front of you driving too slowly? Or were you driving too fast?

Most of us are rushing through the day at full speed. We hit the gas pedal from the time our alarm clocks startle us out of our sleep in the morning. We rush through the day simultaneously, working, texting, typing, talking, reading, meeting and greeting. We eat lunch at our desk or forget to eat at all. We are so busy and preoccupied that we miss the signs that are asking and begging us to slow down, pause, breathe, think and reflect.

The signs are the moments we get stuck in line while waiting to buy our lunch. When we are waiting for someone and they are ten minutes late. When you are waiting for the train and it is fifteen minutes delayed. Life gives us moments to just be. It gives us time to pause and be present for a brief moment. We have two choices, fill these precious moments with, emails and phone calls that can wait until tomorrow. Or we can enjoy being one with our breath. We can even try to fill these moments with gratitude. Allowing the delays, computer crashes and late appointments to be moments when we are grateful for being alive and be aware of the air that we breathe.

Veneration in daily life: Find the moments during your day and embrace the delays. In those moments pause, breathe and be grateful. Taking a pause requires us to explore self awareness so that we are connected to our body and environment. Breathing allows us to take full inhalations expanding our chest and filling our lungs, and full exhalations releasing the tension in our shoulders and allowing our stomachs to soften. In the beginning it may be helpful to count to 4 as you breathe in and count down to 1 as you breathe out and explore your full capacity to breathe and be present with the breath. Gratitude allows us to see the light and joy that surrounds us, reminding us how precious our moments truly are.

To Uplift or Not to Uplift?

*"Let love have a seat between
you and everyone that you
meet."*

I would like to share a story that has been
changed for privacy reasons but still
maintains the essence of the lesson learned.
It was a bright and beautiful Monday
morning. Donna had thought she had cast
away a case of the Monday blues. I think we
all have a case of the Monday blues from
time to time. It's the moment your alarm
clock goes off in the morning and you hit
the snooze button wishing and hoping that
you'll win the lottery, so you won't have to
go back to work and you can have the
pleasure of tossing your alarm clock in the
garbage.

Before she stepped into work she received a
group chat request from her colleagues. She
was excited about the invitation into the
chat group. This was an opportunity to be
accepted, to be included in other outings,
surely, they will invite her to the next lunch
outing. The one she is always excluded from
attending. Finally she thought, I will not be
left alone in the office with my brown lunch
bag. Joyfully accepting the request with
hopes of being accepted she engaged. The

first few messages were about how everyone's weekend went. As she was driving to work the messages began to take a turn. The text notifications were like rapid fire. She began to wonder if people were going to come to work because they were so busy texting. She stopped for gas and began to read the messages. A dialogue of berating and dissecting another coworker began. Let's call the coworker Anne. A dialogue about Anne's appearance and how disgusting they thought she was, began to develop into thoughts of negative words and imagery. Things about Anne that she could not change she was just made that way. Anne no longer was Anne in the chat room she had a nickname based on her attributes. By the time Donna got to work she was deflated and did not want to be at work.

She experienced a series of feelings, which began with disappointment and dismay at the souring of Anne's name. Let's be clear, upon hearing the full story about the workplace dynamic Anne was not perfect, but I think we all know that no one is. No one deserves to be debased. Donna quickly removed herself from the chat group. Every time she tried to delete herself from the chat group she would receive another invite. It got to the point the dialogue was brought to an open forum in the lunchroom. I think we all know what happens next.

Anne walks into the lunchroom, she can hear the laughter and chatter before she enters. She immediately turns around and goes to the bathroom and begins to cry. Donna goes to the bathroom to wash her hands. She finds Anne crying and staring into the mirror trying to muster up the strength to walk back to her desk. Anne and Donna spent an hour in the bathroom talking. What the rest of the team didn't know is that Anne had recently had her third miscarriage and her husband told her earlier, he will be moving out for a while.

Every opportunity we have to engage in conversation with a co-worker, lover, friend, family member or stranger provides us an opportunity to uplift another human being. It also provides us with an opportunity to consciously choose not to uplift the person we are engaging with or discuss the deconstruction of someone who is not present. But wait, there is also a third option. If we are angry with someone or hurt, we have an opportunity to reflect. We can find a lesson in our interactions. Finding the lesson creates an opportunity to grow and continue a relationship of understanding and compassion. This option is not easy. It is often the last resort after days or weeks of stewing. I will be the first to admit that option number three is not always my first choice. I can say this, when you choose option three you can uplift yourself and others while you work through the turmoil. I would like you to embark on today's challenge with me.

Veneration in daily life: Today let's challenge ourselves to create an opportunity to uplift a coworker, friend, child, lover or stranger. Leave a sticky note on someone's desk that says "YOU'RE AWESOME." Or whatever comes to mind. Put a note in your child's lunch box. Leave a note for your lover where they will find it. Just find someone and lift them up today.

When Doubt Creeps In

"Cast out doubt, trust that the love and light within you will take you where you need to go."

It's the moment when you are about to make a major life decision. Change careers, buy a house or end a relationship. When you are ready to share a dream or take a leap of faith, hoping it will all work out. When you are about to embark on a new adventure, you may question if the universe placed you where you are supposed to be and if you were given the tools you need to survive along the way. It's the moments that you are in a room full of people with your big dream on your sleeve and no one has any idea, how you can possibly be happy when you have just a dream in your pocket. When you're surrounded by people who no longer dream, all you can do is keep your dream close to your heart. Take a leap of faith and trust that the universe placed you where you are, to see if you have what it takes to continue on with your mission, when challenges and obstacles present themselves.

I was lucky enough to have a dear friend

who advised me, to read a short well written book. This book is truly something you should keep with you at all times when you are on a new journey with a big dream. This book is filled with many words of encouragement to combat the creeping, sly and deceitful thing called self- doubt. The Dream Giver by Bruce Wilkinson, is a beautiful insightful story about following your dreams and how to overcome the challenges that will arise whether you like it or not. I took my time reading this 156-page book. There is wisdom to reflect on with every page. I would like to share this with you and invite you to read the book.

"...How do I get all my Bullies on my side?"

"Well you might not be able to, Wisdom is the key. Try to understand what's motivating them. Look for the merit of their concerns. Some Bullies you need to simply dismiss or avoid. But most Border Bullies have concerns that can help you clarify your plans. That's how a Dreamer turns

*opposition into opportunity." The
Dream Giver by Bruce Wilkinson*

Veneration in daily life: Find time this week
to write your dream on a piece of paper.
Make a list of what is keeping your dream
hidden on a piece of paper. For every item
listed make a plan to change opposition into
opportunities.

Human Bumper Cars

"As humans we are walking encyclopedias, don't miss an opportunity to learn a priceless lesson just because your ego got in the way."

Every day, while we are on our journeys we are bumping into people. We bump into them with our words, our bodies, our egos, our insecurities, our fears and our souls. Sometimes we are nudged and other times we feel as if someone zapped the energy out of us. We can feel angry, frustrated, sad, irritated, or disrespected. When we allow our fears to create a layer around us we subconsciously build a wall around us. Our fears manifest into insecurities, which can be carried out by our egos and displayed through our body language and words. The fear of not being good enough is at the forefront of many of our interactions. It raises its head in our relationships whether they are friendships, intimate, work related, family or even with people we do not know. The fear of not being good enough can lead us on a winding journey of seeking validation and acceptance. It can create a bumper around us which can block us from having authentic interactions.

If we take a silent moment and focus our energies beyond the physical beings that we present to each other we have the capacity to have honest interactions. Soulful interactions. We have the capacity to communicate with authenticity when we recognize that we are beings of light and love with endless possibilities. When we allow ourselves to see those around us as light beings that are no different from us, we often find that we have a greater capacity to be compassionate, empathetic and present. This allows us to see beyond the layers that we create around ourselves and others and respond mindfully with love.

When we allow ourselves to accept that we are one with all beings, even the ones that we find annoying, we remove the layer of having to be good enough for ourselves and the person we are interacting with. We can create a safe space for one another to be ourselves free of roadblocks and projections.

When I find myself in difficult relationships and on occasions, when I feel like I am being bumped, nudged and winded it can become over whelming. By Friday afternoon I am grateful that I made it through the week but emotionally and physically exhausted. I have come to realize that there is another way. It doesn't have to be about making it until Friday and dreading Monday. During the weeks, where I take the time to meditate, the exhaustion subsides. I realize that I am only emotionally drained when I am stuck, trying to navigate life with my personal layers of self-monitoring and judgment. Searching for answers without taking time to be naked and free from all of my layers. There is a lesson and truth in all of our interactions. Taking time to be silent and present, allows us to peel back the layers and uncover lessons and learning opportunities that assist in our growth and development.

Veneration in daily life: When challenging interactions occur that force you out of your comfort zone, try to find time in your busy day or week to be silent and present with the situation. Trying to be present or meditate can be challenging when you have bumped into someone and you've walked away with a dent. A dent can be holding on to anger or frustration obtained from bumping layers with other people. It can float in and out of the peaceful space you are trying to enter. When the situation floats in you can ask it, what am I to learn or what would you like to teach me? Then let it go. You might not get the answer right away, but over time wisdom and understanding presents itself and the lesson is revealed. You may find that the person who was once annoying or created a volcano of anger within you, is on the same journey as you. A fellow journeyman asking you to learn with them.

Love Thyself

*"Where ever you go love is
with you because it lives in
you. Quietly in every cell and
structure of your entire being
waiting for you to see it."*

Many years ago when I was a young teenage
girl rising and falling at the whim of young
men's love, I had a special moment with my
father that I cannot forget. The message and
life lesson that I learned in this moment has
carried me through many good times and
bad times.

I vividly remember driving down a dark road
in the middle of the night. I had just broken
up with my boyfriend at the time and my
dad came to pick me up. I was crying
profusely. There was silence in the car and
the tears were streaming down my cheeks. I
had felt like someone had taken all of the
love out of my existence. I remember asking
myself quietly if someone would ever want
to love me again. Am I capable of being
loved? Am I loveable? Looking back at these
questions it wasn't the boy that I was hung
up over or crying for. It was the loss of
having someone tell me they loved me,
which made me feel worthy of love. I

remember crying for what seemed like hours. It felt like the longest car ride of my life. I think my dad must have detoured to let me have a moment to let it all out. I asked my father, why does it hurt so bad? I'm quite sure he said a lot of helpful things that floated in one ear and out the other, but there was one thing that stuck all these years. He told me that I can't base my self worth on someone else's perception of me. He told me to get to know myself, and most importantly, learn to love myself, because love lives in me and I was created in love.

I'm not quite sure how old I was when I began to embark on a journey of attempting to dissect and digest this concept of loving myself. I feel like this is something that can take a life time to work on. Eventually I believe it can become a part of your fabric. You may not live and breathe it every day but it can become a part of you that sustains you in the deepest darkest moments. By loving yourself you are loving creation. The best thing about loving yourself is that you can give yourself permission to be as you are.

The love that is inside you is the essence of who you are. You cannot take it away. No one can take it from you even though it feels that way sometimes. You can attempt to hide it with negative thoughts, but it doesn't go away. No one can take the love that rests inside your soul because it is untouchable. They may lead you to believe that love is only there when they express it to you, but it's not true. Love is omnipresent. It is in you around you and flows fluidly throughout you. When you love and believe that you are a creation of the universe. You remove the barrier that often stops us from seeing that we are worthy and greater than we could ever imagine. When you allow the essence of who you are to be free from judgment you blossom and bloom allowing other individual's seeds within themselves to grow.

Veneration in daily life: Tonight before you go to bed and when you wake up in the morning, take a few moments to close your eyes and say to yourself. I love who I am. I Am Love.

Dancing in the Dark

*"Embrace your body and let
the vibration of music put
your life in motion."*

So it's Friday night. Turn the T.V off. Turn
the lights down low. Put your headphones
on, or blast it so your neighbours can hear
and play your favourite playlist. Move your
body and dance. Let yourself get loose. It's
okay, no one's watching. Toss away all the
stress and expectations from the week.
Dance in the middle of your living room. On
your balcony or backyard under the stars.
You can even close your eyes and let the
notes of treble and bass flow through your
body. You might say to yourself this is silly.
Or you might say you don't know how to
dance, but it's okay. Play your guilty
pleasure, songs that you only listen to when
no one is around. Put your pajamas on or
your favourite outfit. Pour yourself a glass
of water or wine and enjoy a Friday night
with just you and your music. Move in a
slow rhythmic motion or leap into the air.

Moving your body provides you with an
opportunity to shift the energy around that
has hung around all week. Embrace your
body and allow it to be free to move

wherever it needs to move. Giving yourself a safe place to let your body be free of judgment gives you an opportunity to have fun in your own skin. Just for tonight fall in love with your curves and how they shift and shake. Love the body your spirit rests in.

Veneration in daily life: Tonight just let go and be free to flow with the vibrations of the music. Let it take you away and get lost with your body.

Dancing in the Love That You Are

"Dance your way into the depths of who you are, there you will find a melodic love song."

Following in the theme of dancing and physically moving our bodies, there are other ways that we can explore dancing in our lives. We can dance internally by exploring our heights and depths, or peaks and valleys. When we take the time to look we may find that the depths can seem so deep, which can be overwhelming at times. We may also find that the heights are limitless with infinite possibilities. If we explore our width, we may find that we can expand as wide as the horizon. No matter which way we explore we are taking a journey to uncover and discover who we are beyond the surface. There is no right place to start, because if we chose to dance within ourselves, gently with curiosity we will find that each step leads us to another step which is in sync with the rhythm of our lives and where we need to be.

Burrowing into our depths can be a scary thought at times. Rummaging through the luggage and boxes that we pack and some of it we carry every day. The other part we may have dug a deep hole and placed the boxes into the earth hoping that we would never find them again. If we start with the luggage we carry around with us every day we can begin to unpack it. It's like when you have planned a trip for 5 days and you pack 10 pairs of shoes. One for the day and a different pair to change into every night. Or ten shirts just so you can have variety. When you return home with your luggage and you begin to unpack, more often than not you have shirts that you didn't wear and shoes that never touched the soil at your destination. It is possible that you brought your most comfortable shoes and you probably wore them the entire trip. You have a moment where you realized that the extra baggage fee that you paid for when you checked in to bring the extra luggage that you tagged along with you just in case you needed it wasn't worth it. So when you plan your next trip you may just pack two pairs of shoes and six shirts, because you are only willing to pack what you need and now you are lighter, simply travelling with a carryon bag with no extra fees.

By unpacking our personal luggage that has an emotional cost or stagnant energy that creates a feeling of being stuck, we create the possibility of travelling through life a little lighter and clear with focus. There is no guarantee that we will never have luggage or baggage when we travel. If we set time aside to unpack our luggage once in a while we may find that little by little our load gets lighter. Some things we will re-pack and that's okay, and some things we will look at and wonder why it is still lingering and toss it away. We can create opportunities for our boundaries to be clearer and what we truly need to be present with us when we are faced with challenges. There is nothing wrong with having baggage, at times when it gets to heavy there is a moment where we can be mindfully curious and begin to evaluate the value assigned to the heavy load in our lives.

We may unpack and dance when we arrive at our destination which is the present moment. The one where we decide to take a look at where our feet are planted. Dancing in places we've danced before and sometimes take the same steps time after time. Wait that's a song... Depending on what song is playing in our lives, some steps in our dance routine may have to go and some are just a part of our style that makes us who we are. We are not limited to dancing in one direction. We can dance and explore our heights and dreams within. We can dance in ways we have never danced before, which can force us to take steps out of our four step comfort zone.

It all starts with a dream and one step at a time. This is when we can think about dancing with passion. What is it in our lives that creates a sense of soul connection? It could be a job, task, hobby or way of being, and every time we jump in and begin to do it we feel that it is part of our purpose. Sometimes we might even say we don't know what it is but this feels right. If we follow that intuitive voice within us it will guide us to the first step in making our dreams come to fruition. By the time we look back we may often find that the steps into the unknown were choreographed and rhythmic with the flow of our life.

Invite yourself to take a trip and dance and sway in the flow of your life where all things are possible and all routines, lead you to growth and infinite possibilities. Sometimes it's hard to think about dancing when your feet feel like they are trapped in cement blocks. Or we feel that if we start to dance someone will judge our style and form. The longer we sit at the side of the room listening to our favourite song play we allow the fear within us to build up, and now our song has ended. The good thing about songs is that you can always press replay or change the beat.

Veneration in daily life: Look within and ask, where are my feet? Where do I want them to be? How much am I paying for my extra luggage? These are not easy questions and they may not be answered in one hour, one day, one month, or one year. If we answer just one of them, it will take us one step into choreographing our dance within.

Consciously Transforming

"There is great power in the words we speak and write, use them to craft the route to your destination."

I recently purchased a book for $6.50, and it was the best six dollars and fifty cents I've ever spent. Wisdom and awareness can be found on each page of this book. Paramahansa Yogananda (1893-1952) wrote Scientific Healing Affirmations. I would like to share one except from this book. I believe it can be applied universally to all people wherever they are on their journey. These few words provide insight into how powerful our words are. We often hear people talk about changing our internal self-talk. We speak about changing how we communicate with others. Rarely is there conversation about why we should change the way we communicate with others and ourselves on a soul level. Yogananda captures the essence and passion from where our motivation to change how we communicate can grow and expand from.

"Spoken words are sounds occasioned by the vibrations of thoughts; thoughts are vibrations sent forth by the ego or by the soul. Every word you utter should be potent with soul vibrations. A man's words are lifeless if he fails to impregnate them with spiritual force." (Yogananda, 1981)

He has broken down where our words manifest. We are often busy in our daily lives. Rushing to keep up with the fast paced flow of the world we live in. We are often communicating with more than one person at a time. We are texting, while we are speaking on the phone or in someone's presence. We are sending emails while we are in meetings or out for lunch. We are feverishly completing tasks while we attempt to meet our social needs. The ability to multitask is phenomenal. It allows us to believe we are being efficient and effective and have a sense of accomplishment at the end of the day.

If we take a moment at the end of the day to tally up how many people we had contact with and communicated with we would be surprised. Each time we say, "Hey how are you doing?" and don't wait for a response as a part of our interactions. Each time we say hello or send a business related email can we truly say it is done with intention and purpose? Have we allowed our soul to communicate our passion and impregnate it with spiritual force as Yogananda stated? Or have we allowed our ego to block the flow from our soul and communicate on our behalf? It is an interesting concept that is worth contemplating. What would life be like if we tried to fill every conversation or opportunity to communicate with spiritual force?

Veneration in daily life: One day this week, try to start and end the day with having conversations infused with purpose. Get beyond the surface.

Comfort Zone

"When we release the chains of our comfortable discomfort we create room for the impossible to become our reality."

Today I was introduced to the following quote. It created a well-needed shift and a shove into awareness and out of distraction.

"People have a hard time letting go of their suffering. Out of a fear of the unknown, they prefer suffering that is familiar." Thich Nhat Hanh

---

If you take a moment to think about what this quote means for you in your life right now, the energy of fear may be present in your life, which can force you to stay in your comfort zone. There is nothing wrong with staying in your comfort zone. It is cozy and warm. You know what to expect and when to expect things. The challenge is how long can you stay in your comfort zone? What form of suffering have you allowed yourself to be comfortable with? And what fear is blocking you from living a life of soul purpose?

We can stay in our comfort zone as long as we have fear blocking us from experiencing something new. Common fears that keep us in our comfort zone are the fears of rejection, inadequacy, not being loveable. Sometimes we can become so immobilized by these fears that we will endure suffering because even the suffering can become comfortable and predictable. We may even endure the suffering to validate our fears of rejection, inadequacy and not being loveable. We may isolate ourselves from getting to know others because we fear the potential of the relationship not going well or being rejected. We may stay in a relationship that is intimate, work related or a friendship even if it is toxic and harmful to us just to please someone else. While embracing the fear that you are not loveable and should you end the relationship you will be alone and no one else will want you, should it be an employer, lover or friend.

The good news is that the Universe will force us at some point to get out of our comfort zone whether we like it or not. All we have to do is trust that it will catch us in the way that we need to be nurtured on our journey. Even better, we have the power to get out of our comfort zone and work past our fears. In order to take this step we have to be able to be honest with ourselves. Be free to say what we are afraid of. If we find ourselves in a relationship or environment that is not conducive to our well being we have to give ourselves permission to ask ourselves, why are we there? And what is stopping us from changing the circumstance?

Veneration in daily life: Think about what is in your comfort zone. Asking the following questions may help identify the fears that are blocking change. When am I suffering? Where am I suffering? How am I suffering? Why am I suffering? What fears are validated by my suffering?

Navigating a Perplexed Matrix

"Let your intention be rooted in love and the rest will be a history you will want to repeat."

There are many ways to look at and assess human nature. We can view it as a song and dance, navigating through the rhythm of a song that we think we may have chosen. We can also look at it at times as a tug of war, waiting to see who will collapse first. At times when we look at it from the ego we never really get the full picture. If we perceive that we have the upper hand and there is someone to conquer, corner or overcome we begin to be short sighted. Through the lens of the ego it is easy to attempt to wage a war. In order to perceive that someone or something is conquerable, we may have to hold the belief at some point along the way that someone or something is less than. When we begin to see one another not as equal, but as sub-human or less intellectually capable than we are, we have already lost the war. Fumbled our steps in the dance or forfeited the game of tug of war.

We can find this way of being in many facets of our lives. One could argue that being discerning would be the answer. But then you have to ask the questions. Does bringing fear to war ever win a war? Perhaps not, I'm certain history can demonstrate this. No one truly wins when history writes about a winner or a loser.

If we approach one another from a genuine place of love, not a romantic love but the love that is in the essence of who we are. The part of us that may continue on beyond our physical mold cast out of flesh, could we live a more authentic life? If every act of kindness was done from a place of love, not lack, or need, could our interactions be elevated?

Veneration in daily life: Intentionally try to engage in life from a place of agape love, while alleviating lack and fear as a guide to surviving.

Choices and the Inevitable Ripple

"For me and my brothers and sisters are one, every choice I make has an impact beyond what my mind can conceive of."

Every choice we make has the ability to change the course on which we are travelling. Every choice we make, and I would argue every thought has the capacity to send a ripple into the universe and impact what is to come in our lives and those around us. There are choices every day that we make, some are small and others are big but they all leave a footprint, which determines where we take our next step. We have a choice to be kind when we are faced with un-pleasantries. We have a choice to love when we are faced with fear. We have a choice to follow our spirit or our egotistic motivations. No choice is right or wrong but each one sends us on a journey of twists and turns. At times it may be difficult to make a choice at all. We may find ourselves caught between our consciousness and our wants derived from living in lack of. Both are valid and both have a place because they are all a part of us.

So what do we do when we are caught in a dilemma, where we can't see the light at the end of the tunnel? When what we want, desire and truly need conflict and we are not quite sure what direction to turn, we can ask the Universe a question with soul intention. We can ask the Universe to point us in the direction that aligns with our soul's purpose. I can honestly say that each time I've ever asked this question the sea parts and the direction reveals itself. I would be lying if I said I went willingly 5 out of 10 times, more like 2 out of 10. Whenever I have looked back after the dust has settled, the way presented itself, but it is clear that I may not have been as ready to receive as eagerly as I was fast to ask.

Now the true challenge presents itself. Are you truly ready to accept the insight that you were presented with? If you are, then you may embrace the path that has presented itself. It doesn't mean that it will be smooth sailing but it could lift the weight off of your shoulders. Okay maybe some of the weight, but there is an indescribable feeling that comes over you that lets you know you are in the right place, for you at that moment on your journey.

We may find ourselves more than we would like to swimming against the flow. So we ask the beautiful creation we call the Universe to shed light and wisdom upon our narrow tunnel that feels unbearable. The next thing we know there is a bright star shining a light and leading us out of the tunnel. Our legs get heavy, we become full of fear and we try to lift one leg toward the light. It doesn't budge, we wiggle and fight. We can even feel the warmth of the light touch our skin but we struggle with that first step. The struggle we experience is with what we wanted the answer to be and the answer that has revealed itself. We can convince ourselves that the warmth on our skin that is shining upon us doesn't feel good. Simply because we are not ready to let go of what we wanted and ready to accept where we need to be, in order to align with our true path. If we open our hearts, we may allow the fear and comfort in our fear to subside and let us catch up to the insight we asked for.

Veneration in daily life: Ask the Universe to guide you in the direction that aligns with your soul's purpose. Stay open enough to embrace the revelation with love.

New Beginnings

*"Let the seed of life within
you flourish and blossom into
a beautiful rose bush, with
fragrant flowers and newly
sprouted buds."*

New Beginnings

It's in the air and flowing among the trees.
Whispering into ears.
Dancing in visions and enticing with
missions.
Begging and pleading to take flight in
endless skies.
Running and racing in lessons and lives.
Uprooting and levitating with many
goodbyes.
Steering and twisting on streets that are
becoming alive.
Shedding scales and injuries from past
journeys.
Finding a new place to lay roots and
foundations.
Fearless and free from bullies and thieves.
Prancing and skipping new steps to new
beats.
Bobbing and weaving in realms and
philosophies.
Awakening and breathing light into souls.
Enchanting new eyes with new visions that
are bold.

Jumping and leaping without supervision.
Loving and freeing sounds of bliss.
Creating and manifesting new words that
have been missed.
Travelling and soaring at rapid speeds with
beings up high.
It's time for a new beginning.
New dreams of infinite possibilities beyond
our finger tips and eyes.

When we embrace a new beginning in our
lives we can invite the beginners mind to be
our partner along the way. Giving us a fresh
set of eyes to see the world and explore
situations familiar and new.

Veneration in daily life: Take a moment to
sit with a situation that is currently
occurring in your life. Bring a fresh set of
eyes and mind with an open heart. What
are possible outcomes that could uplift
people involved based in compassion and
kindness?

Words of the Heart

*"True love is recognizing and
nurturing the light within the
one you desire."*

In the era of Internet dating and texting we
have rejuvenated literature and the art of
the word. We have recreated ourselves and
the best version of ourselves in the form of
words. We often condemn this way of being,
but it has allowed the art form of wooing
with language to have a place again. People
will often write each other for months and
years before they actually meet in person
and embark upon their first touch of
physical intimacy. This is not much
different from the time when people would
write love letters to one another. The only
difference is that we have the speed of light
to take these messages to and fro. In the
past we would wait weeks on end and have
a lengthy bout of anticipation upon
receiving a letter and getting lost in the
thoughts of a lover.

The beauty of writing letters is that
someone had to take the time to craft a
thought create imagery, confess and divulge
their soul and intimate desires. The person
receiving the letter could re-read the letter
until it got tattered and torn. There was

time to explore the feelings that the letter created uninterrupted and without the expectation of responding with minimal thought or effort. So why write a letter or leave a note instead of a text? A text is quick and easy. It's to the point and gets the message across instantly. At times texting can feel like instant gratification. The longing for becomes short winded and short lived. We have mere seconds to create a mood and atmosphere, to set a tone, which, due to the expectation of responding quickly often gets lost in translation. If someone doesn't respond quickly we become anxious or begin to think the worst, forgetting that people are often texting while they are living their lives far removed from having time to explore their intimate thoughts undistracted by life's busy demands. We can shift this way of communicating by sending letters or notes from the heart by any medium but with deep intention straight from the heart. I found this note to be endearing yet simple. It expresses a sense of longing for without the expectation of a response. It just is and it's beautiful.

Dear Stranger,
The moment I laid eyes on you, it was clear to me that you are a creation of the divine. I realized what love at first sight truly meant. I could hear the sounds of Etta James singing

At Last gently into my eardrums as if it was the soundtrack to my life. I bump into you every now and again, but I don't think you see me the way I dance in your scent and energy at the mere passing of you. Time passes and I find myself drunk in the remnants of your aura long after you're gone. When you say hello, I can swim in the tone of your voice. Time stops for a moment and all is well. These words may never find your heart as it belongs to another. But I'm grateful to dance in the warmth of your energy at a moment's glance or simple hello. From: Love from afar.

Veneration in daily life: Write a love letter or note. It can be fiction. It could be for someone you are dating, married to or someone you met once and hope to meet again. Or it could be for someone that you hope to meet one day. Take time and write a letter. Whether you mail it or not, just enjoy uninterrupted time to explore your feelings of love and desire fearlessly.

Caress My Soul

*"I never knew what it was
like to be loved until she
caressed my soul."*

I have been fortunate enough to meet a
woman who I would call magical. She could
make you a cream to help you through the
excruciating pain of childbirth, and it
actually work! She could heal a god awful
chronic pain without a touch. She could
calm you with her soothing voice when feces
hit the fan. She brought joy into the room
with her laughter. Most of all she cared for
people beyond the flesh. When you were her
friend or even acquaintance you knew that
you had an opportunity to be in a
relationship with someone, who cherished
the experience of getting to know you. She
mothered you and loved you just because.
She had a fire inside of her that could fuel a
city for years. I was lucky enough to know
her for a short period of time in the flesh.
I'm now left with thoughts and whimsical
moments, where I know she's there without
a doubt. Her life was too short and I think
everyone who knew her, would say that they
miss her greatly. I miss her greatly!

She was the kind of friend that would drive

for 2 hours and sit in traffic just to bring you, your favourite meal from a little shop across town. Because she knew, that before giving birth and while having contractions, a care package from the little family owned restaurant that knew you well, would make you a special concoction to comfort you. She was the kind of person who would come to your house, when you're all alone on your birthday with a new born with no idea what to do, but feel absolutely lost. She would come over make you a cake and give you a pep talk that gave you fuel to decide to sign up for a second language while you were on maternity leave. She would give all of herself to you and you would do the same without a second thought.

She fought for women she knew and women she didn't know, but I think she also fought for herself. She made changes for women on a journey where domestic violence would try to break and dismember their sense of self. She would say when she was a child until she grew into a woman that her family's nickname for her was, Joan of Arc. I would say that was true to who she was, well maybe with a little mother earth and fairy dust in there too. She fought for women even when she was being abused. She stood on the top of the hill and fought for what she believed in, even when there were people gnawing at her flesh. It's hard for me to fathom that she was abused by the men who were close to her. It's even more difficult to comprehend how such inner and outer beauty and grace could be overlooked, or attempts made to destroy and discredit a loving being. I would be lying if I didn't admit that I also saw women attempt to do the same. Yet through all of the trials and tribulations she still chose to shine.

There was one partner that she met later in her life, who was truly able to see her for who she was. When you were blessed enough to be in their presence, you knew there was a soulful love in the room. They made you believe in love again. They were soul mates. When they would embark on healing you, they had this symbiotic spiritual synergy that danced together flawlessly. At the celebration of life ceremony that was held for my dear friend her partner stood up before a room full of people with his drum. It was a moment that I will never forget. I think the entire room cried in unison. Not just a regular cry it was that kind of cry where you can't be bothered with where you are or who is around or what you look like. I can't remember exactly what he said, but I do remember these four words that has taught me something profound. *"She caressed my soul."* I believe he said that she truly saw him, and he never knew what it meant to have someone caress your soul until he met her. He then slowly and steadily beat his drum.

These four words have opened a pathway in my life. It has allowed me to believe in the infinite possibilities of love. It is possible to experience having a soulful relationship with another being. It is possible and we are worthy of wanting and experiencing a loving relationship that touches the essence of who we are. I think we are familiar with the phrase, *"many are called but few are chosen."* I would say that in matters of the heart this phrase can be applied. Many will knock at your door and masquerade in variation of the dance of love and desire, but it is up to you to choose the one that wants to dance with you, not in front of you. Dance with someone who not only caresses the small of your back yet takes the time to delicately nourish and caress your soul.

Veneration in daily life: Ask yourself, where is love in my life? What does love look like in my life? What do I want love to be like in my life?

Letting Go

"Letting go is a process that allows us to evolve and grow."

When do we let go? How do we begin to let go? As we travel on life's journey there are sunny days, rainy days, thunder and lightning storms, weather warnings, tornadoes and even earthquakes. I believe the Universe will send us gentle rain showers and place us in the eye of the storm at times. You may drive through the rainstorm or travel the distance and ignore the weather warning. The reality is, you cannot ignore the earthquake that is off the Richter scale. You cannot ignore being stripped of all layers that we project to the world, and being left with nothing but the essence of who you are. The moment when you are standing in the middle of the rubble that is left after the earthquake and there is no one, or no structure left as it was. You look around and no one quite understands what or who you lost, because changes in the flow of our lives are unique to each and every one of us.

These moments may feel awful but they offer you an opportunity to look within and ask yourself, if all that I need is within me then where do I go from here? I believe the answer is anywhere! In order to be able to explore infinite possibilities and the gifts of the earth shattering change that left you with nothing but the clothes on your back and the soul in your body, you have to be ready to let go. Until we remove the limitations that we create which block us from manifesting and exploring life to our true potential, we will limit ourselves from relocating to higher ground.

I enjoy quotes from all walks of life as each path brings light to a truth. There are two quotes that resonated with the theme of letting go this week. The first quote lays the foundation and the second quote prompts you to take action.

"To everything there is a season, and a time to every purpose under the heavens: A time to be born, and a time to die; a time to plant, and a time to pluck up that which is planted..." Ecclesiastes 3:1-2

> *"Now is the time to consider the things that no longer serve you, and to let them go, just like the leaves dropping from the trees. Whether it's resentment, sorrow or a need to please, we all cling to things that ultimately hold us back, and it's now time to reflect and figure out how to let these things go and move forward."* unknown

I think when we look deep within we know when it is time to let go. We know when it is time to leave a relationship, a situation, a way of being, and a job. There is that feeling inside of you that says enough is enough. The part of you that begins to detach and once in a while raises the question, why am I still here? Whether it is with him or her, here or there, or behind a desk. At times it could be that we still have a few lessons to learn, but when we have witnessed the lesson occur more than once and we have walked through the fire and allowed ourselves to learn and be reborn, then it's time to start considering letting go.

Today I am going to let go of the beliefs that don't serve me.
Today I'm going to let go of the expectations

that don't serve me.
Today I'm going to let go of the suffering that doesn't serve me.
Today I'm going to let go of the matters that do not speak to my soul.

Veneration in daily life: What are you trying to let go of? What is stopping you from letting go?

Desire

*"Embrace your sexual energy
and allow it to live amongst
you, freeing it from the
shadows of shame."*

How often do we talk about desire? I believe
that it is far and few between. There are few
honest conversations between intimate
partners, friends and lovers that openly
create space to discuss desire. Desire is a
powerful energy. There are so many people
living in this world who are too afraid to
admit that they have fantasies and
thoughts that are not confined to a box. We
wait until books come to the mainstream
like 50 Shades of Grey to feel comfortable
talking about sexuality and fantasies.
Meanwhile we've been doing this long before
books and movies.

It is a part of our reality that we have desire
as a part of our thoughts and needs. Too
often, we quiet these thoughts out of shame
or embarrassment. The more we quiet these
thoughts in our intimate relationships the
more our needs go unmet. We also silence
intimacy when we don't honour our own
bodies and believe that we are beautiful and

desirable beings. We yearn for someone to desire us, yet at the same time most of us cringe when we look at ourselves in the mirror. We want our partner or someone to say I want to get lost in your body. Yet when it happens, we look at them and say, this body? Really? And we look around as if they weren't talking to us.

Let's listen to Sexual Healing by Marvin Gaye. It is a well-known song and probably in this day it will have many labels and hashtags attached to it. There is a truth in this song. He talks about not beating around the bush. It encourages us to enjoy the song and dance of intimacy shamelessly and freely. He talks about the spiritual connection between sexuality and the spirit within you being moved and awakened. It's not just a fantastic timeless song, there is much to learn from it if we really listen to what he said.

One of the challenges that comes to the surface when we have the need to be desired, requires us to delve into our inner sexual energy and evaluate where it is. Is it deep within afraid to come out? Is it bubbling on the surface ready to flow like a waterfall? When we find where it is we can ask ourselves, how do we pull it out and set it free, and how do we honour it so it is sustainable. We can start by nurturing and loving ourselves and believing that we are desirable from within. A lover can only love you or explore you as much as you love yourself or are willing to explore yourself. If one believes this from within then external validation is mere confirmation of what you already know and believe, which allows you to be free from attachment upon being validated. Yet it is possible if we do not believe this from within then external validation becomes like a delicious piece of cheese cake. Your mouth begins to produce saliva when it is placed before you. You devour it quickly and then you are left with an empty plate and a yearning for more. Meaning that when we solely rely on external validation to stir our sense of desirability then we open up the door for an intensity that is not sustainable. We set ourselves up to further live in a deficit.

Another perspective which is valuable is the idea of making space and acknowledging desire. I had an opportunity to watch a TedTalk featuring Ester Perel. She encourages you to take a look at your own desires and the ability to create erotic space in your relationship. She has also written a book Mating in Captivity, which provides much insight and prospective.

Veneration in daily life: Would you be willing to share your fantasy with your partner? Do you feel desirable? Make a date with yourself and safely explore your sexuality and desire.

New Year of New Moment

"Reflect, renew and release.
On the night of New Years
Eve let the shadows cast
away and light of your soul
rise."

Happy New Year! The reset button has been selected and we now have 365 days to do something awesome! If you want to write a book, you could commit to writing every day for 30 minutes. If you want to improve your well being you could commit 20 minutes a day to meditation. Now I have just committed 50 minutes of your time, multiplied by 365 days... well that's a lot of time, math has never been my strong point. I would like to bring a few pieces of wisdom that friends and family have shared with me in 2014 that I would like to bring into the new year.

1. Be your own best friend. We are often able to give advise and provide insight to our friends and family, but it becomes challenging when we have our own issues. You can ask yourself the following: If my best friend was in this situation what would I say to her/him?

2. Approach life with an open heart and from a place of love. Approaching matters whether it be work, friends, relationships with an open heart creates a space to remain authentic and remove a layer of judgment from a situation.

Approaching life from a place of love is a step into living without fear. Love has the ability to overpower our fears. At times when someone says something hurtful to us, we have an urge to become defensive and continue the hurtful exchange of words and energy. By continuing this negative exchange, we make a choice to live in fear. Fear that our respect has been compromised. Fear that someone may have power over us. Fear of being left behind. Approaching a situation with love provides you with the ability to position yourself in a place where you can respond with care. The reality is hurt people often hurt people. By responding with love you don't own someone's hurt, yet you shift the vibration of the energy exchange.

3. Follow your dreams. The road may get bumpy. There may be a sudden road closure diverting you to an alternate route that you have never taken before. You might even be forced to take a break and get a tune up followed by an oil change. After your break get back on the road to your

dreams. We all have dreams and it's up to us to keep them alive and take the road less travelled to get there.

May the new moment or year bring you growth and opportunities to explore the world you live in and who you are.

Veneration in daily life: Imagine you are your best friend, what would you say to yourself about a current situation that is a source of stress?

What is Trust if We Don't Trust Ourselves?

"Trust that the divine wisdom is always present within you to guide you. Make time to be still and listen."

Trust is something that most people place on a pedestal in our relationships with others. We often make statements like the following.

"You can trust me."
"I trust you, I hope this stays between you and I."
"You can trust me, I would never hurt you."
The challenge with these statements is that they require an action. If the action and behaviour were present, would it be necessary to make the statement?
Then we can delve into what trust means to us. Trust can mean the following. You trust someone to be reliable, honest, sincere, abide by their word. You trust someone to be supportive, attentive, respectful of your feelings and dreams, and mindful of your relationship and its growth and

development.

Today I was asked, what is trust in a relationship? My initial response was, trust is when someone is able to commit to their word. It is knowing that you are free to be your authentic self. Trust is when you have space to express yourself without judgment and it is received with warmth.

Then I was asked, what is your relationship to trust? I think that my relationship to trust is within me. I trust that I am who I am. I trust that I will love myself regardless of my failures and successes. After I answered these questions I was told the following. "YOU DON'T NEED TO TRUST ANYONE BUT YOURSELF!" I sat with this phrase for quite some time. I think it might sit with me for a few more days. I am beginning to think about the concept of trust in everyday life. We often say to our partners I trust you to be faithful. I trust you to honour me and my way of being. I trust you to be there when I need you. And then we tack on for the rest of our lives! If we take a look at all three statements, we are really asking and at times begging someone to be trust worthy and letting them know that there is a price to pay if they do not follow through with our expectations, which makes us feel like we have control over their actions as we made our potential outcomes clear.

The challenge is we can only be responsible and take ownership for our own actions and actively exercising trustworthy behaviour. In order to begin building trust with ourselves or others we can consider two concepts. I would love to say that this is an original thought but it is a product of an amazing course that I am taking right now.

1. Congruency: Say what you mean and mean what you say! If we allow ourselves to be clear about our intentions by being sincere with our word, then we can avoid the slippery slope of manipulation of our own thoughts and manipulation of others. When you mean what you say and say only what you mean you create space for honesty and authenticity.

2. Consistency: If you say you're going to do something you must follow through on it. No matter how big or small it is. When we consider following this we can also ask ourselves, do I truly want to follow through? If the answer is no, we can consider if it is something we should say at all.

When we consider our personal relationship with ourselves and the concept of trust, we can ask these questions, do I trust myself? Can I trust myself to love me when I succeed and when I perceived that I have made grave mistakes? Can I trust myself to have my own back? It all comes back to self love. If I love who I am within, I can trust that all I need is within me. I could evaluate how I use the notion of trust in my relationships and question whether it is authentic and realistic.

Veneration in daily life: What does trust mean to you? How do you create trust in your relationships and with yourself?

Out with The Clutter

"At the end of a play the actors bow and leave the stage. Let the actors in your life go and prepare for the next show when their scene is over."

At the end of the day when you finally have a quiet moment to think about what happened. When you can reflect on the moments that took place in the busy day, it is easy to start thinking about what worked, what was uplifting and what was exhausting. Lastly what sucked the life out of you. I often wish that there were more uplifting moments in the day. Some would say you have to look for them. I am quite grateful when they land in my lap. It is evident that at times in our lives there is an imbalance in the battle between uplifting moments versus sucked the life out of you moments. There is an imbalance between people who are willing to be brave and genuine and those who seek your energy, time, and mind at convenience. An imbalance between living and pushing through the routine out of being comfortable and being alive and taking on tasks that touch your soul. An imbalance between people around you who allow you to grow and live without judgment and those who smile, yet you can feel the vibration of judgment and insincerity lingering in the air. The discord created within when you do what is comfortable discomfort for a living versus doing what you love, that which makes your heart sing. So what stands in between us and living the life that we want? I'm beginning to believe that it is clutter!

The clutter that is created when we hold on to old beliefs. The people that we entertain who suck our time and energy, the ones that we know if we just said no that they would quickly find another being to ingest. The negative thoughts that can lead us down a dark road. The job that pays the bills but depletes you unforgivingly. The busy life style that doesn't give you time to be grounded, just present enough to check off a box on your long list. I'm sure there are a lot of ways to demonstrate clutter, but here is the thing about clutter. It can and will take up space in your life in rooms and sheds that you had planned to use for something else. It will linger like stagnant energy until you feel stifled. Sometimes we don't want to get rid of the clutter because we have attached a memory, feeling or sensation to it. We don't want to hurt someone's feelings by discarding their clutter that they are storing in your place.

You do have the power to get rid of the clutter. It can be scary to wonder what life would be like with open spaces and room to dance and sway as you please without hitting a box or energy that would make you slip and trip. If we honour the soul that is within us and look within, getting rid of the clutter is really creating space for the essence of who you are within to shine unobstructed.

Veneration in daily life: Do you have clutter in your life? What are you willing to get rid of?

Blend In or Be Awesome

"I am worthy of living my life in complete expression of who I am."

" If you are always trying to be normal you will never know how amazing you can be." Maya Angelou

---

These words of wisdom offer so much depth and provide an opportunity to percolate on how you want to explore your potential. It is very easy to fall into the sinkhole that is "...trying to be normal..." Blending in so you won't be noticed or trying to be normal to avoid having other people feel awkward or uncomfortable. Or doing it out of fear, fear that the real authentic you won't be accepted, because if the real you full of life and gifts, things you cannot change is not accepted then the sinkhole of trying to be normal gets deeper and lonely.

There is something alluring about trying to

be normal. At times it can create a sense of security, a bond, friendship, a sense of approval and belonging. The challenge is when bits and pieces of your authentic self, starts to seep out of you at the seams, it becomes difficult to maintain blending in. You may begin to feel that the foundation of the relationships around you, may not be as stable and secure as they once were. The spirit within you may begin to fight for space and opportunities to be free. As this occurs it becomes evident to yourself and those around you that you aren't normal, you are in fact quite unique. Some people begin to run away like you have the plague, others may keep a safe distance to allow them to be curious yet untouched by your light, and some may take your hand and embrace the beautiful spirit that you are and ask you to dance.

Each and every one of us have the right to explore how amazing we can be. Sometimes it can be hard to do when it feels like there is no room or tolerance for you to be true to who you are. The truth is, where ever you sit or stand is a place and space that is your own. There is no road or special place to begin exploring how amazing you are. There is no special time or situation you must wait for to allow your gifts to shine. There is no special person that you need to wait for, to affirm that you are special beyond measure. You can begin anywhere, because where ever you begin there is love everywhere ready to embrace you.

Veneration in daily life: What are your special gifts? Are you trying to blend in?

Pieces of the Puzzle

*"With each life lesson we
receive a piece of the puzzle
that helps us to get a better
glimpse of the bigger picture.
It is worth working through
the lessons."*

Here we are in this life, living, loving,
laughing, crying, dying, growing and being
reborn. We are all searching for something.
Searching for that piece of the puzzle that
gives us a glimpse of hope, of the future,
and confirmation that we are where we are
suppose to be. Some pieces we receive do
not fit at this moment in time. But we put
them aside so we know where to find them
when it's time for it to click in. Some pieces
look like they fit, and we spend time trying
to squeeze it in but it just does not feel
right, but we know it fits somewhere. There
is an undeniable feeling when the piece of
the puzzle is presented to you and the
moment it slides in perfectly, you gain
perspective and insight to the bigger
picture.

There are so many paths that we can travel
to find pieces of our puzzle. We may never

find all of the pieces in this life time, but it does not mean the journey is less significant. It gives us a chance to feel, and experience the lessons and beauty in our darkest and brightest moments. As we travel on our journey there are many things that we will take with us and many things that may help us discover our route. One of the valuable tools we can take with us is keeping our hearts open to explore through conversation. When we have an opportunity to engage in conversation about our life and experiences we have the ability to create a space that allows energy to flow and exchange. Through this exchange knowledge and wisdom are shared and insight presents itself as our puzzle pieces.

Veneration in daily life: Allow yourself to be open and create a judgment free arena to indulge in conversation about where you are at on your journey and explore the jagged edges and curves of the next puzzle piece.

I Will Be Happy When?

*"Happiness is the state of
your inner being, align your
state of mind."*

Today the universe knocked on the door
and said two things. Okay I think it's more
than two but I can only comprehend and
decode a few knocks at a time. Before I
share them, I really think it is important
that we take time to acknowledge all of the
people in our lives. The ones who challenge
us and makes us frustrated, angry,
annoyed, and force us to experience lessons
that we try to avoid. The people who are
living their lives in the flow of love and
share wisdom, insight, joy and infinite
possibilities with you. The people who have
experiences for you to learn and grow from,
your mentors, guides, friends, teachers. The
unseen who are your cheerleaders whether
you can hear and see them or not. Your
family whether they are the people at this
point you would have chosen to be a part of
your life or not, like it or not they have
helped you to be who you are today. Maybe
you did choose them but...perhaps we
forgot. I think that could be another
reflection on its own.

The person at your favourite go to foodie spot that has your order on the go from the time you walk into to the store because they took the time to get to know you, even if it is for brief moments, that is their way of showing they care. I'm sure I could go on and on. Here is the thing all of these people and beings are reasons to be grateful. While on my journey a few of these wonderful people have been knocking on my door.

I once heard someone say. You are different and special. You are different from many amongst you. You are not better or less than, you are just different. Once you accept, 1. That you are different and you must embrace who you are.

2. People around you may not accept you or understand you and it is okay. We are all on different paths and it is okay.

We are all filled with many things that make us unique and special. We all have a special craft, whether it be painting, writing, dancing, managing, counseling, creating furniture, whatever it is we know when we do it, we feel like we are free to be who we truly are. One of the challenges that we experience on our journey of self- discovery is that the more we become free and authentic and accepting of ourselves, we are challenged with a great lesson. Can you be your authentic soulful self when you encounter the masses that will say you are not enough, or too much, or you don't fit in? Can you continue to be yourself when doubt creeps in? Can you still treat them with love and kindness even though they may twist your kindness because it's unfamiliar to them? I truly believe once you can say yes you will experience new growth that will guide you on new flourishing paths of discovery.

Acceptance of ourselves can translate into our experience with happiness. When I get that job, or start that career or meet that man or woman, when I finish that degree, when I win the lottery, when I save up enough money to go on that trip, when I can buy that car, when I can, has the ability to go on forever. When I do X I will be happy, but until then, I will be unhappy and allow this unsatisfied existence to bleed into my life and drain me. If that sounds familiar I think it's because we all do it in some shape or form. If we can accept who we are at this very moment, we will realize that we can be happy just as we are. It is easier to travel on our journey when we remove the limitations of X.

A wise man once said to me. Your spirit is always full of love, joy and happiness. It is your mind that believes it is not happy. He suggested that if we can make more time to meditate and get in touch with our spirit, we may find that happiness comes from within and it is always with us.

"Joy lives abundantly with you. It is the mind that tries to convince you otherwise." Dr. Ghartey

---

Veneration in daily life: What is your X?

Hidden Gem

"After the storm passes walk along the shore and you will find many hidden gems that have been brought to the surface."

There is often a secret gem in an experience that initially appears to be negative. When a partner leaves us, you get fired without cause, or a friendship ends. All three situations force you to peel away all the layers that may have allowed you to stay in a situation that was comfortable discomfort. As you peel back the layers you uncover a spectrum of emotions, memories, expectations, and old boundaries. You wonder when the moment of foreshadowing took place in your life. The moment that read a narrative that said this relationship is not forever. The moment you knew it was time to move on yet you ignored it, hoping things would get better.

Then the moment comes, that you can't avoid. Your partner sits you down and tells you it isn't working anymore and they walk out the door with their bag packed. So what do you do next? Well the truth is you may spend a day, a few weeks or a month in bed. Wearing your pajamas and hiding from the world. You may not shower every day or you may binge on Netflix. Okay and perhaps there may be a lawyer involved over time depending on your situation. But after you get through the initial phase of grief and loss. You may start to see a glimmer of the hidden gem under all the hurt as you unearth it. When you get time to find yourself again because the distractions have removed themselves out of your life. You will find peace, freedom and who you really are again.

Perhaps you get rid of the old boundaries that didn't serve you. The one's that allowed you to ignore the gut feeling that bubbled up from time to time resulting in heart ache or heart burn. You toss out the expectations that glued you to the ever after and that things would get better. Perhaps you allow the positive memories to be stored away and you reflect on the negative memories for a few moments to continue to dig for the gem as you transform pain into triumph through uncovering life lessons. As you take a few moments, or days to ponder on the moments that felt unpleasant, you may feel emotions rise, anger, sadness, and a bout of passion for correcting injustice may arise.

So what do we do with these feelings? As we

feel the energy of these feelings become strong and take over our being. We have the ability to channel this strong energy and transform it into sustainable fuel to allow us to take charge and live the life we always wanted. You will be amazed to see how much you can accomplish when you channel your energy towards something that nurtures your well-being.

Although the end of a relationship or situation can be painful it has a purpose. It is the universe telling you that your lesson here or there are done, and it's time for you to enter a new path. A new chapter, a new way of being. It's time to get in touch with your purpose here on earth. It is okay to look back, but do not look for too long. The universe gave you a gem. A limitless fresh start.

Veneration in daily life: What led you to unearth your hidden gem?

Unlocking The Door

"The key to your door is within you. You were born with it."

In our life there are many doors that we encounter. Some are closing, some are opening and some require the right time and moment to reveal what is on the other side. Some doors are even locked until that moment. Not because someone locked us out but because we locked ourselves out. At times, we may lock ourselves out of our creative minds and areas that we may have silenced out of fear or an experience that left us wounded.

I'm going to tell you a personal story about a dear friend of mine and how she helped me unlock my creative door through art. Okay just to be clear she is my creative partner in crime who I am very lucky to dance with in the creative flow. She is a phenomenal woman, who I am so grateful to know. And most of all an amazing friend. She is creating a beautiful collection of doors. One of my favourite doors that she has created is the image that appears below. Go to her website to learn more

about her beautiful
creations. https://threadbareart.wordpress.
com

Created by Heather Gailey

The universe allowed Heather and I to
collide at a place where we both worked.
Her and I started by saying hello and having
a warm exchange of smiles. These warm
exchanges quickly led to discussions about

spirituality, infinite possibilities and art. At the time, Heather was teaching art journaling once a week. Once a week Heather would have her materials for her workshop in her car ready to go after work. I have kept journals for years, I have journals from elementary school, but the pages have always been filled with words and maybe a scribble or two of hearts surrounding my name and my crush at the time. Heather introduced me to the world of Art Journaling. Before I met her I never thought about the possibility of having art in my journal or using art as my medium to journal. In my eyes she was sharing her creativity just as freely and natural as it came to her. She told me about her creative journey and I began to tell her about my creative past, as if it was a part of me that I had locked away behind a door never to be seen again. I didn't realize it at the time but I think Heather might have caught on, so she invited me to spend our lunch break one day that week painting.

I told her about a tale of a diverted journey when I wrote poetry and bravely read it at a restaurant on open mic nights. I was creating music and teaching piano and began teaching my neighbour's child how to play. I was freely expressing myself until I had a moment that led me to subconsciously and physically seal the door. One afternoon I was preparing to sing and play a song I wrote for the next open mic night. I was determined to overcome my fear of playing piano and singing at the same time and the second fear was performing in front of an audience. That day while I was practicing someone came up behind me and said, "It would be so much better if you stopped singing." So I stopped as simple as that. I didn't attend the next open mic session, and slowly over time I stopped playing and I only wrote in my journal that I kept hidden in my room.

For quite some time the door to my creative expression was closed. No one closed it for me not even the person who didn't enjoy my singing. I closed the door and decided to step back into my comfort zone. My comfort zone began to take over. When I met Heather years after this experience I had created a uniform for myself, a uniform which represented a refined containment of my artistic expression. I had turtlenecks in black, blue, red, white, pink, and purple. To be honest I had about five in black and one in each colour listed. Followed by two pairs of black pants. There is nothing wrong with a turtleneck or black pants but I was using it as a shield. A major part of me was missing and it was easier to hide behind my uniform than ponder on what was missing.

When Heather suggested we explore painting and Art Journaling on our lunch break, I was a little nervous as it was quite some time since I shared a creative space with anyone and my medium has always been writing and music. My mother can sew anything from a wedding dress to an apron, my aunt is a painter and photographer, my brother studied fine arts in university, my uncle is a sculptor and my grandmother was a seamstress. I come from a long line of creative people but I never thought I could paint or create an image that expressed my thoughts and feelings.

The day finally came, Heather and I used the entire hour of our lunch. Within the first 15 to 20 minutes I watched Heather take a blank piece of paper and turn it into a beautiful expression of who she was at that moment in time. She was layering and mixing colours effortlessly. She brought paint brushes, stamps, and showed me how she used recycled objects as stencils. I looked down at my piece of paper and wrote peace, love and creativity with a watercolour crayon, something I had never used before. Heather told me that I could get a little bit of water and smudge the letters and just let the colours blend. I looked at Heather's masterpiece and I looked at my three words and I smiled. As simple as they were, those three words came to life. In that moment

Heather created a safe place that was loving and peaceful where we could explore our creativity. That was the moment that the door to my creativity was unlocked. It is amazing how art can heal wounds and open doors. I went home that night and cut up my turtlenecks and hung up my black pants.

Veneration in daily life: Have you ever unlocked a door? What did it feel like?

The Sun Will Rise Again

*"When we lay our bodies
down and feel submerged by
sorrow, remember that the
sun will always rise and lay
its rays upon us tomorrow."*

In the moment when a catastrophe strikes
and you can see the world, as you know it
slipping away, it might not be completely
gone from your fingertips but you have been
awakened to the possibility that life could
change drastically. There is no reason or
purpose that we can make sense of in that
moment. We may cry until we have no tears
left. Our fears begin to play out in our
minds like a movie that we told ourselves
we would never watch, because we knew it
would give us nightmares.

We don't know what to say when people
gather around us and we don't want them
to see how unraveled we are on the inside,
but the truth is we need them. We need
their optimism and even hugs, not to tell us
that it is all going to be okay. But we need
them to let us know that in this moment if
we fall or lay on the floor and cry that they
will lay beside us for a little while. After

some time has passed they will outstretch their hands to help us get up.

Life can change in the blink of an eye or after a good night's sleep, or while you are doing your day-to-day routine. You might not be able to see it after your worst fear becomes your reality, but with one foot in front of the other, one out stretched hand at a time you will find life after that moment. I can assure you that it won't be the same, but I do believe that you can live again. One day you can wake up and watch the sunrise like it was the first time you had ever seen it.

Veneration in daily life: Who held your hand after a catastrophic event took place in your life? Call them and thank them, or if you see them, give them a hug.

The Many Hats We Wear

*"Authenticity is when we
allow our entire being to shine
brightly as it is."*

As we travel on the road that is our lives we
will discover parts of ourselves that we may
not have known. Or perhaps there are parts
that we have put to rest until we have the
energy and desire to explore them. At times
old parts might come to life and shine
brighter than we could ever imagine. These
parts are often represented as hats that we
wear, the way we present ourselves to the
world. We may acknowledge that we wear
different hats depending on the occasion or
audience. We put on the nurturing hat for
our children, the pristine employee hat at
work, the erotic lover for intimate partners,
the wholesome hat for our families and the
list can go on and on. We flip our hats on
and off with ease as if the body beneath it is
an empty vessel, only activated upon the
need of an audience or task.

There is a possibility to consider, the hat
can only be worn if the attributes already
exist within. If the hat is only a decoration
of what is truly inside, parading the

highlights of our depths, then we may only end up sharing and exploring the surface of who we really are. It may be worthwhile to explore the depths of the body that models our best hats, because there is more to who we are than the decorations that appease our audience or get the job done.

Regardless of how many times we change our hats in a day or week, the essence of who we are does not change. Just as the seasons may change, the essence of the earth remains beneath our feet.

Veneration in daily life: Make a list of all the hats you wear. What hat do you wear the most? What does it feel like when you put it on? How do you feel when you lay it to rest for the day?

Moments

*"Sparks of joy and magic are
happening all around us.
Take a moment to pause and
be a witness."*

There are so many moments that pass us
by. Not only the moments that happen in
our lives but the beautiful moments that we
are a part of and witness while we are in the
presence of others. We often focus on the
big moments. The wedding day, buying or
renting our first place, first day of school,
graduation, and annual celebrations. There
is so much happening in between that we
need not look too far and we can be filled
with joy by being present in someone's
moment. I truly enjoy people watching. You
learn so much about human interaction
and subtleties when you sit back and allow
real life in motion to be your movie.

My motion picture that moved me consisted
of watching two people meet for the first
time. I watched the light hues of rose rush
to her cheeks every time the young man
would speak. How she smiled and turned
her head when he looked at her avoiding
eye contact. I watched her engage him in

conversation when she became comfortable. This all sounds quite simple yet it is powerful. By being aware of the moments that are happening around you, it becomes evident that inspiration is not found at some special places, or only on movie screens or perhaps require you to pay for them.

I watched my son as he viewed his favourite cartoon. His beautiful smile and at times a look of concern came across his face and then fluctuated to laughter. I witnessed how dynamic and beautiful he is which brought me joy.

There are beautiful moments all around us. Life may not be perfect, and finding joy could feel hopeless at times. Remember there are millions and billions of magical sparks happening around us simultaneously. Just take a moment to look around and you will find one.

Veneration in daily life: Take a moment in your day. Stop for 5 minutes. No computer, no screens and be present in the moment. Use your senses to look around. What did you find?

Take a Pause and Shift Your Attention with Intention

"Be true to who you are, even when they say you're too much."

When you wake up in the morning and begin to prepare for your day at work a countdown begins, timing how long it will be before you put on your professional hat. The hat that says I'm ready to get down to business and do whatever it takes to get the job done. The hat decorated with peace symbols and flowers if your way of survival during the workday is keeping the peace. Or perhaps you put on a hard hat to protect you from the fecal storm that seems to never end. Regardless of what kind of hat you place on your head when you begin to work, the hat is decorated with your feelings about the work environment and who you may need to be to survive in it. Expectations of you from your coworkers and the person you would like people to see when they interact with you. All of these expectations create a lot of pressure and inconsistency in our lives. So let's take a moment and look at Susan.

Susan has been working at a high profile marketing company. There are several cliques at her place of employment. Her boss is a part of one of the groups. In this group there are three other women who share the same values as her boss. Susan does not share the same values. She is reluctant to become a part of the group but believes that she will not get a promotion unless she adapts to the culture and business values of the group. The thought of conforming is troublesome to her as it creates an internal struggle and disconnect from who she is and who she may need to be. Susan's boss and the group make it clear to Susan that in order to be successful and increase her bonus for the year she must do whatever it takes to make a sale. This includes telling the customer what they need to hear, making an offer that will not be beneficial to the client in the long run, and significantly reducing the amount of time spent with a client to maximize numbers and sales.

A few weeks ago Susan was confronted with another challenge while she spent her lunch hour with this group. Comments were made about cultural stereotypes and the role of people in the company. A derogatory comment was made on several occasions about the cleaning staff and people who do not reside in areas that are perceived as affluent. It took Susan a few months but she adapted to the business culture. She decorated her hat with qualities and characteristics that were not natural or authentic to who she was. Her language with customers became direct and Susan's relationship with her boss and co-workers improved. She would force a smile when comments were made that were uncomfortable. By the time she got home she was exhausted. The amount of energy it took for her to fit into an organization that did not share her values was overwhelming, as she had to wear a hat that did not fit just right.

A great question for Susan would be, are you working at the right company or department? Unfortunately, Susan's hat does not resemble the person underneath it. It's a reflection of a costume not an augmentation of her authentic style. It is often that we find ourselves in these situations. If you make the same choices as Susan, you may end up with a closet full of hats that you don't really like. Susan's boss may move on and the group of coworkers may disperse into different roles. If Susan doesn't become comfortable representing who she really is or perhaps not wearing a hat at all, she will always feel exhausted trying to wear someone else's ideas and values.

Veneration in daily life: Are the qualities you're projecting at work based on who you are or who you think you need to be in order to obtain success? Are your values consistent in all areas of your life? What would your day at work look like if you showed up without your hat?

How Can We Get Out of the Mud?

"Take a pause and shift your attention with intention."

The workday could feel really long. Especially if you have skipped lunch or didn't take a break because you were in the flow. The week could feel even longer when it's only Tuesday and you're asking your colleagues if it's Thursday. I think we all know what that feels like. I've listed seven affordable and short activities you can do at work that will give you a little break during the day and switch up the gears that may need to be changed.

1. Go for a walk outside. If it's cold do a lap in the office or climb the stairs.
2. Keep a vase on your desk. Nothing fancy, any bargain vase. Purchase flowers and leave them on your desk until you need to change things up. Take 5 to 10 minutes and make a flower arrangement at your desk.
3. Listen to an upbeat party song that always gets you moving. Suggestion, put your headphone on and take a 3

to 5-minute dance break. This might take a little bit of courage if you don't have your own office or a closed off cubicle. Dancing in your chair will do. If your boss is open minded perhaps they may encourage you to take the headphones off and ask everyone to stand up and participate in the party. Your selling feature to your boss is that the average song is only about 3 to 5 minutes. Everyone will be pumped up and more productive. If you're the boss well then include it in the workday for all.

4. Doodle! You are never too old to doodle and you don't have to have an artistic bone in your body. There are several books on Zen Doodling. All you need is a blank piece of paper. If you want to be green, use the other side of paper that you plan to shred for the day.

5. Make a list of five things that you are grateful for and post it on your desk. Or make a virtual sticky note on your computer. This is a perfect activity when you get the mid- week blues.

6. Google writing prompts. Complete the first one that you lay your eyes on. Set a timer for five minutes and write. If you love writing you might want to keep writing. If you want to keep writing set the timer tomorrow for

another five minutes and continue the story.

7. Keep an inspirational book on your desk. Open it to a random page and take a few minutes to read the page. Does it relate to your day?

These are just seven inexpensive activities you can do while at work. Bring a little joy and creativity to your day and have fun.

Veneration in daily life: Try one activity a day. Or try the same activity for one week. What do you currently do to break up your day? Make a list of things you would like to do.

Reflections of an Open Heart

*"Peace is present within you
at all times, create moments
for stillness and you will find
it has always been there
waiting for you."*

As we travel along from one experience to another, some experiences reveal lessons the moment you step into it. And others may reveal the lesson days, months and perhaps years later. When the revelation of the lesson is delayed we often beat ourselves up and wonder why it took so long. We may even say to ourselves that the lesson was so obvious that we could have avoided it all together. That is usually our ego driven inner critic that speaks up in those moments. When we receive the lesson does not matter, it is more important that we allow ourselves to be open enough to learn it.

There are so many emotions we experience in the process of learning a lesson. We experience anger, it thrashes and slashes out of us while we scream and shout, why is this happening? We point fingers and blame while we convince ourselves we have found the culprit. It becomes challenging to get out of this way of being and it becomes more difficult to believe that we could move forward with our lives without the anger as our anchor.

We may also experience sadness. Sadness that cuts deep within us and reaches a new found unhappiness that we did not think was possible. We convince ourselves that if we do not carry this sadness with us, that showers us with tears then we did not care enough.

Fear becomes present within us, wondering what would life be like after we walk through these emotions. Our fear keeps us spinning our wheels in the wet mud. One of the questions that are frequently asked is how do you get out of the mud?
One way is meditation. You may say, geez who isn't saying that meditation is the way out. Everyone under the sun is raving about meditation. And...they should be! Meditation is not about having some amazing adventure into a different realm. It is about finding stillness in the midst of anything that allows you to be present and realize you are connected to everything. Meditation awakens you to the realization that you are more than your body. Coming

to terms that you may be more than your body could be a life long journey of exploration. Meditation gives you a gentle nudge and reminder of this possibility. It is quite easy to get sucked into the emotions that become so concrete that they create a wall blocking us from stepping forward. Having a brief moment where you experience being more than your body can disconnect you from the emotions of anger, sadness and fear. This release can reveal many valuable lessons.

Veneration in daily life: Meditation is an amazing tool that is free. Set aside 15 minutes today to seek stillness.

Unconditional Love

"When my heart is open, fear cannot be present to misguide me."

What does it mean to be open? This is a really good question that can generate an abundant amount of responses. When we strive to make an effort to be open, the door starts from a tiny crack that allows a little bit of light to come in, then it becomes half way open. When it becomes half way open, you may experience moments where you question whether striving to live with an open heart is worth it. You may stand before someone with your arms and heart wide open yet they close the door leaving you on the other side. This can happen more than a few times. By the third or forth time you may become disenchanted. The sadness that fills you when the door is half open provides you with an opportunity make a choice. You can close the door and close your heart, and the ability to experience while being present. Or you can continue to open the door until the door comes off. Allowing your heart to be fully open to experiencing love in all forms and experiences that you never thought were possible.

Close your eyes and visualize for a moment. Imagine yourself standing with your arms wide open as if you are trying to give someone a hug. Imagine a big ball of light around you representing the love and light that you are. Now imagine someone standing in a doorway across from you. Their hands are by their sides, yet they are looking at you. You begin to send a beautiful bright beam of light from your heart to theirs. They receive a bit of the light and then close the door. The light from your heart continues to flow but now it's flowing back to you as it bounces off the door. Are you not still surrounded by love?

Whether someone decides to be open to your love or not, thankfully it does not determine the amount of love that surrounds you. You are love, therefore you are always abundantly surrounded by love. A very beautiful teacher once said the following. "You can never love too much." When you send love into the world or to someone, it may not come back directly from your source of intention but it does come back to you in many unexpected ways.

Veneration in daily life: Silently send love into the world or to someone from your heart today. Imagine a large beam of light extending from your heart to theirs.

Creating Goals From Within

*"True love has no boundaries;
it is not controlling nor can it
be confined."*

When we speak of unconditional love it has depth and power. When we live it, it has the power to change our worldview and the lives of others around us. By choosing to dig into the depths of unconditional love for ourselves first, means that we are growing to release ourselves and those we encounter from judgment. We can make room for forgiveness in our lives for ourselves and those who hurt us.
We can start with little steps every day.

1. Start your day with love. Look in the mirror when you wake up in the morning and say to yourself, "I love all of you. Every mark, scar, and curve. You are brilliant, beautiful and full of joy." Create your own saying that ignites your light within and gives you the fire to get through the day. Say it out loud until you feel it within.

2. Tell at least two people during the day that you love them. You can write a note, send a card, write a meaningful text or call them on the phone.

3. When you are speaking to someone and your internal voice begins to negatively speak about them, stop for a moment acknowledge the thought and say to yourself, "I may not agree with you but I will listen with love."

4. Make a choice to interact with your co- workers, family, and friends with the intention of seeking to support their well-being and the greatness within them.

5. Love yourself regardless of the choices your make during the day that you perceive as mistakes. Take a moment to consider what you may have learned or gained from the experience.

Unconditional love is the act of mindfully placing love as the foundation of your thoughts, decisions, actions, business, communication and daily life. Relationships will blossom and die. People will enter and exit our lives as the seasons of our relationships change we can still make a choice to make love the foundation of these transitions.

It is not about being perfect yet giving yourself space to forgive and still love yourself, even when you make choices that are out of alignment with love, your purpose, passion and personality.

Veneration in daily life: Take a moment to reflect today. Is there someone that you are currently having a disagreement with? Close your eyes and visualize the person and the situation. Imagine it being resolved with love. What would that look like?

Love, Meditate, Reflect

*"Love, Meditate, Reflect,
Visualize & Motion."*

Five easy steps to create goals from within.

Apply Love!
Are you thinking about making a change?
Whatever your goal is, take a moment to
apply love to it. How do I apply love to my
goals? By viewing your goal through a
loving lens. Does this goal align with my
purpose? Does it contribute to my wellbeing
and the wellbeing of others? Does it ignite a
fire within me that inspires me to be the
best version of myself? Applying love
doesn't stop after you answer these
questions. It's applicable throughout the
entire process of achieving your goal. It is
practicing having compassion and being
gentle with yourself, throughout the
challenges and opportunities to learn that
may occur, while you are striving towards
your goal.

Pause and Reflect!
Take a moment to reflect on where you are
going, where you have been, who you went
with and who you don't want to go with.
Sometimes we can get lost in the sea of

events and people that surround us. Stop and take count of where your feet are planted, and take a good look around with your eyes open and heart ready to see your truth.

Bring Clarity!
Sometimes our goals after the first few weeks or months become a little muddy. The inner critic has made their opinion known. People around you may have made suggestions. Our challenges or we could call them opportunities to grow, seem a little insurmountable. Take a moment to enter the space of stillness within yourself. Take a few minutes a day to allow your mind, body and spirit to be present through meditation. By practicing meditation, we can develop the ability to quiet the constant internal and external chatter and shift our muddy waters into still waters.

Create It Within!
Many people have said, start how you would like to end. We can do that by visualizing our goals. When you set your goals visualize your intended outcome. What would it look like when this goal is completed? Make it colourful. Take a few minutes in the morning or before you go to sleep at night to visualize your goal. After you visualize your goal write it down just as you saw it within your mind's eye. If we can see it, we can

conceive it.

Put It into Action!
It's time to manifest! Take your intention and desire and make a Mind Map or an outline that demonstrates your action plan. With every step you may want to ask, does this bring me closer or further away from where I want to be?
Have a wonderful time creating! Anything you want to do is possible. Allow your dreams and purpose to guide you. Let your light shine, and illuminate others as you go along on your journey.

Veneration in daily life: Is there something that you have always wanted to do? Write a book, turn your hobby into a career, find a way to reduce your stress? Take a moment. Close your eyes, take 10 deep breaths in. Ask yourself, what would a successful wholehearted completion of this goal look like? Start creating!

Find your light and illuminate your journey. And together, let's find our light and illuminate the world.

May you explore your greatness and shine your light bright for all to see.

About Randi-Mae

Randi-Mae is a Personal Strategist, assisting individuals, couples and organizations with exploring their potential and dreams while integrating wellness practices to enrich their wellbeing. She dedicated five years of her career in service to the community as a frontline Crisis Support Worker. Through assisting individuals in some of the most challenging moments in their lives she was able to discover that everyone has a journey, and is worthy of being heard, seen and supported. In 2015 Randi-Mae brought her dream to fruition and created Inspired Journeys with the assistance and support of her community. Her services are provided on four principles; love, meditation, visualization and motion. She graduated from the University of Guelph-Humber with a Bachelor of Applied Science Degree in Family and Community Social Services and

a diploma in Social Service, and
has acquired training in wellness coaching,
mindful meditation, tai chi, and domestic
violence safety planning and risk
assessment. Randi-Mae is happy to share
her personal journey which is filled with
challenges, loss, growth and resilience. She
believes that if we can share our journey
with one another, we can illuminate a spark
within someone else and give them the
courage to start and continue theirs.

www.randimae.com
info@randimae.com

Thank you

Thank you mom for all of your assistance, support and guidance throughout the creation of this book. Thank you dad for loving me. Thank Jelani Daniel for sitting me down and telling me to commit and follow through. Thank you for being a messenger. Thank you so much Sue Paré of Susan Paré Eformatting Services. You are an writer's dream angel.

Thank you to my supportive family Bruce and Dianne Leibold for believing in me and supporting me. I appreciate you so much. Thank you Zeke for coming into the world and showing me what it is truly to love and want to make the world a better place. Graham thank you for giving me the space to create. Thank you Karl for being my loving protective brother. Thank you Lorraine for being my family I didn't know I had. Thank you Janine for finding on my first day of school. Thank you Evette, Carol, Jean for being my aunties who are fierce and determined. Thank you Celina for seeing me in a moment where I thought I was invisible. Thank you Pedro, Nahida, Lee, Heather, Morgen, Sarah, Neil, Shereen, Kofi, Mr. Wang, Ellen, Jon, John, Esther, Priya, Jamie, Tina, David, Andrea, Helen, Jordan, Kennita, Ms. Sokoloff, Linda,

Kathryn and Kiana and many more beautiful people who teach me, love me and support me.

Thank you to all beings of love and light who guide me, connect me and ground me every moment, of every day. I am truly grateful and honoured.

Thank you to all of the people who came before me who allow me to live and breathe in this moment in time.

I am truly grateful.

www.ingramcontent.com/pod-product-compliance
Lightning Source LLC
Chambersburg PA
CBHW031626040426

42452CB00007B/703